Primary Sources in U.S. History

The EXPANDING FRONTIER

Enzo George

Cavendish Square

New York

Published in 2015 by Cavendish Square Publishing, LLC
243 5th Avenue, Suite 136, New York, NY 10016

© 2015 Brown Bear Books Ltd

First edition

Website: cavendishsq.com

CPSIA compliance information: Batch #WW15CSQ.

All websites were available and accurate when this book was sent to press.

Library of Congress Cataloging-in-Publication Data

George, Enzo.
The expanding frontier / Enzo George.
    pages cm. — (Primary sources in U.S. history)
Includes index.
ISBN 978-1-50260-248-0 (hardcover) ISBN 978-1-50260-247-3 (ebook)
1. United States—Territorial expansion—Juvenile literature. 2. West (U.S.)—History—Juvenile literature. 3. West (U.S.)—Discovery and exploration—Juvenile literature. I. Title.

E179.5.G468 2015
978'.02—dc23

2014026354

For Brown Bear Books Ltd:
Editorial Director: Lindsey Lowe
Managing Editor: Tim Cooke
Children's Publisher: Anne O'Daly
Design Manager: Keith Davis
Designer: Lynne Lennon
Picture Manager: Sophie Mortimer

Picture Credits:
T=Top, C=Center, B=Bottom, L=Left, R=Right

Front Cover : FC All images Library of Congress
All images © Library of Congress, except; 10, © Bettmann/Corbis; 30, © Shutterstock.

Brown Bear Books has made every attempt to contact the copyright holder.
If you have any information please contact licensing@brownbearbooks.co.uk.

We believe the extracts included in this book to be material in the public domain.
Anyone having any further information should contact licensing@brownbearbooks.co.uk.

Manufactured in the United States of America

CONTENTS

INTRODUCTION

Primary sources are the best way to get close to people from the past. They include the things people wrote in diaries, letters, or books; the paintings, drawings, maps, or cartoons they created; and even the buildings they constructed, the clothes they wore, or the possessions they owned. Such sources often reveal a lot about how people saw themselves and how they thought about their world.

This book collects a range of primary sources about the westward expansion of the United States, from the late eighteenth century until the 1890s. It focuses on social and cultural history rather than political issues such as slavery.

Even before the United States was created, pioneers began to cross the Appalachian Mountains to the Ohio Valley. With the purchase of the vast Louisiana Territory from France, expansion began in earnest. By the 1840s migrants were crossing the country by wagon train, spurred by "manifest destiny"—a belief that U.S. expansion was both inevitable and justified. Native American peoples were displaced to make way, until their armed resistance finally ended late in the nineteenth century. The coming of the first transcontinental railroad in 1869 marked the age of the "Wild West," but within twenty years the frontier had vanished: the United States now spanned the entire continent.

HOW TO USE THIS BOOK

Each spread contains at least one primary source. Look out for "Source Explored" boxes that explain images from the 19th century and who made them and why. There are also "As They Saw It" boxes that contain quotes from people of the period.

Some boxes contain more detailed information about a particular aspect of a subject. The subjects are arranged in roughly chronological order. They focus on key events or people. There is a full timeline of the period at the back of the book.

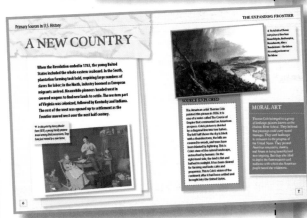

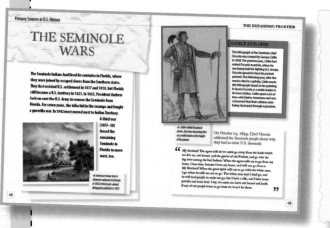

Some spreads feature a longer extract from a contemporary eyewitness. Look for the colored introduction that explains who the writer is and the origin of his or her account. These accounts are often accompanied by a related visual primary source.

A NEW COUNTRY

When the American Revolution ended in 1783, the young United States included the whole eastern seaboard. In the South, plantation farming took hold, requiring large numbers of slaves for labor; in the North, industry boomed as European migrants arrived. Meanwhile, pioneers headed west in covered wagons to find new lands to settle. The western part of Virginia was colonized, followed by Kentucky and Indiana. The rest of the West was opened up to settlement as the frontier moved west over the next half century.

▼ *In this print by Henry Mosler from 1870, a young family prepare to eat among their possessions. They have just moved to a new home.*

◀ *The full title of Thomas Cole's picture is* View from Mount Holyoke, Northampton, Massachusetts, After a Thunderstorm—The Oxbow. *It is usually just known as* The Oxbow.

SOURCE EXPLORED

The American artist Thomas Cole painted this picture in 1836. It is one of a series called The Course of Empire that commented on American progress. Cole's picture is divided by a diagonal line into two halves. The left half shows the sky is black with a thunderstorm, the hills are covered in woods, and trees have been blasted by lightning. This is Cole's view of the natural landscape, untouched by humans. On the right-hand side, the land is flat and bathed in sunlight. It has been cleared for farming and looks calm and properous. This is Cole's vision of the continent after it had been settled and brought into the United States.

MORAL ART

Thomas Cole belonged to a group of landscape painters known as the Hudson River School. They believed that paintings could carry moral messages. They used landscape to comment on the progress of the United States. They painted American mountains, deserts, and forests as being beautiful and awe-inspiring. But they also liked to depict the determination and resilience with which the American people tamed the wilderness.

NATIVE AMERICANS

▶ This image shows a Native American hunting buffalo. Both were under threat from U.S. expansion into their territories.

The new United States was home to hundreds of Native American tribes, some of which had lived in North America for thousands of years. Many Native Americans had never come into contact with colonial Americans, but the nineteenth century would bring a complete change in their lives. By 1850, many of the traditional customs of the tribes had disappeared. Some tribes died out thanks to disease, alcohol, or conflict. Those peoples who survived were moved from their tribal lands and forced to live on reservations.

In 1787, Chief Pachgantschilias of the Delaware warned Delaware converts to Christianity about Europeans:

" I admit that there are good white men, but they bear no proportion to the bad; the bad must be strongest, for they rule. They do what they please. They enslave those who are not of their color, although created by the same Great Spirit... They would make slaves of us if they could; but as they cannot do it, they kill us. There is no faith to be placed in their words. They are not like the Indians, who are only enemies while at war, and are friends in peace. They will say to an Indian, 'My friend; my brother!' They will take him by the hand, and, at the same moment, destroy him. And so you will also be treated by them before long. Remember that this day I have warned you to beware of such friends as these...
They are not to be trusted. "

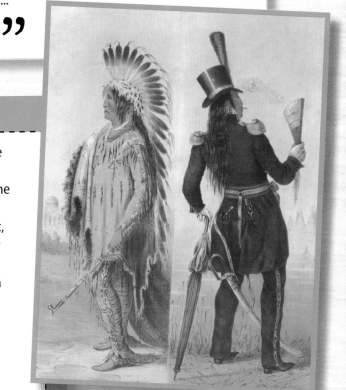

SOURCE EXPLORED

This picture was painted by George Catlin in 1838. It shows a Native American named Wi-Jun-Jon. On the left he is going to the White House to meet the president. On the right, Wi-Jun-Jon is returning home after the meeting. He has given up his traditional dress; he wears Western uniform and carries a fan. Catlin is suggesting that the deals Native Americans made with the U.S. government came at the price of giving up their culture.

▲ Catlin's image was published as a print in 1838 by the famous New York publishers Currier and Ives.

DANIEL BOONE

▲ This lithograph from 1874 illustrates an episode in which Daniel Boone had to protect his family from a Native American.

One barrier to U.S. expansion was physical. For centuries, the Appalachian Mountains prevented pioneers moving west. In 1775, however, Daniel Boone created the first wagon route through what was known as the Cumberland Gap. Boone and his frontiersmen blazed a trail, later known as the Wilderness Road, into what is now Kentucky. By the end of the eighteenth century more than 200,000 settlers had crossed the mountains to a new life in the Ohio Valley.

SOURCE EXPLORED

This picture was painted by George Caleb Bingham in 1852, over 75 years after Boone crossed the Appalachians. It reveals a lot about nineteenth-century atttitudes to the West. In reality, the crossing was challenging for Boone's fontiersmen. The painting shows settlers, including women, making an easy crossing. They are bathed in light. This shows them as a "civilizing" influence in the dark, savage landscape. The men's guns suggest that they are ready to fight in order to settle new lands.

AN AMERICAN HERO

Daniel Boone was an early example of a new American hero: the frontiersman. In 1784 a book decribed Boone's life on the Frontier, wrestling bears and fighting Native Americans. Many of the stories were made up or exaggerated, but Boone became famous. His courage, independence, and ingenuity were characteristics that many early Americans believed were the foundations of the new country.

◀ *George Caleb Bingham painted* Daniel Boone Escorting Settlers Through the Cumberland Gap *long after Boone's original expedition and his death in 1820.*

THE LOUISIANA PURCHASE

Thomas Jefferson became president in 1801. In 1802 he asked the French ruler, Napoleon Bonaparte, to sell New Orleans to give the United States control of the Mississippi River. Instead, Napoleon offered to sell all of Louisiana, which covered most of the American Midwest. The Louisiana Purchase of 1803 pushed the U.S. border west to the Rocky Mountains.

▼ The port of New Orleans in Louisiana gave the French control over the Mississippi River until 1803.

▼ *The map was accompanied by two sheets of information about the location of French troops.*

SOURCE EXPLORED

This map of the area around the Mississippi River from Lake Erie to the mouth of the Ohio River was drawn around 1755 (north is in the top right corner of the map). It is thought to have been created by a Native American named Chegeree and a British official. At the time, the British were concerned about the French presence in the Ohio Valley. But Europeans knew little about the interior of the continent, so Chegeree's information was invaluable.

On April 18, 1802, Thomas Jefferson wrote to Robert Livingston, a U.S. official living in Paris, about the importance of buying New Orleans from the French:

❝ Every eye in the United States is now fixed on the affairs of Louisiana. Perhaps nothing, since the Revolutionary War, has produced more uneasy sensations through the body of the nation. Nothwithstanding [although] temporary bickerings have taken place with France, she has still a strong hold on the affections of our citizens. I have thought it not amiss, by way of supplement to the letters of the Secretary of State, to write you this private one, to impress you with the importance we affix to this transaction. I pray you to cherish Dupont. He has the best dispositions for the continuance of friendship between the two nations. ❞

LEWIS AND CLARK

▶ This illustration of Lewis and Clark holding a meeting with Native Americans was published in 1810.

After the Louisiana Purchase, Jefferson asked the army veteran Meriwether Lewis to explore the possibilities for river transportation in the new territory. With his friend William Clark and a corps of explorers, Lewis set out on May 14, 1804, up the Missouri River from St Louis. After eighteen months crossing the continent, making maps and noting everything they saw, they reached the Pacific Ocean. Their efforts opened a new overland route for settlers to the Rocky Mountains and beyond.

On September 22, 1805, Meriwether Lewis recorded meeting the Nez Percé after a difficult crossing of the Rocky Mountains:

" The pleasure I now felt in having tryumphed over the rockey Mountains and decending once more to a level and fertile country where there was every rational hope of finding a comfortable subsistence for myself and party can be more readily conceived than expressed, nor was the flattering prospect of the final success of the expedition less pleasing. On our approach to the village which consisted of eighteen lodges most of the women fled to the neighbouring woods on horseback with their children, a circumstance I did not expect as Capt. Clark had previously been with them and informed them of our pacific [peaceful] intentions towards them and also the time at which we should most probably arrive, the men seemed but little concerned, and several of them came to meet us. "

SOURCE EXPLORED

This map was engraved in 1814 to accompany the official history of the expedition, and was the first map to give accurate information about North America beyond the Mississippi River. Clark shows a tangle of mountain ranges. They ended Jefferson's hope of finding a navigable river route across the country.

◄ This map was based on the many maps made by William Clark during the journey and was engraved by Samuel Harrison.

THE WAR OF 1812

On June 8, 1812, President James Madison declared war on Britain. There were various causes. They included the British capture of U.S. ships trading with France, with which Britain was at war, and British support for Native Americans in Canada who were hostile to the United States. Canada was the main battleground, but the largest battle came in January 1815, when a British defeat at New Orleans led to the end of the war.

▲ This U.S. cartoon criticizes British alliances with Native Americans. It shows Native Americans taking U.S. scalps on behalf of the British king, George III.

▲ Only the walls of the mansion were left after the fire, and nearly all of them had to be pulled down and rebuilt.

SOURCE EXPLORED

On August 24, 1814, British troops, commanded by General Robert Ross, marched into Washington, D.C., and set fire to the President's House, the Capitol, the Navy Yard, and several U.S. warships. This colored aquatint was created at the time by the engraver William Strickland. It shows the damage to the President's House, which was not yet known as the White House. It also shows how empty this part of Washington still was nearly twenty-five years after it became the U.S. capital city. On August 25 a huge rainstorm put out the fires, preventing more damage. Many of the city's public buildings were later reconstructed in the form we know them today.

AS THEY SAW IT

66 The flashes of lightning seemed to vie in brilliancy with the flames which burst from the roofs of burning houses, while the thunder drowned the noise of crumbling walls... The consternation of the inhabitants was complete, and to them this was a night of terror. 99

—British soldier George R. Gleig describes the attack on Washington, D.C., on August 24, 1814.

THE SEMINOLE WARS

The Seminole Indians had lived for centuries in Florida, where they were joined by escaped slaves from the Southern states. They first resisted U.S. settlement in 1817 and 1818, but Florida still became a U.S. territory in 1821. In 1835, President Andrew Jackson sent the U.S. Army to remove the Seminole from Florida. For seven years, the tribe hid in the swamps and fought a guerrilla war. In 1842 most moved west to Indian Territory.

A third war (1855–58) forced the remaining Seminole in Florida to move west, too.

◀ *American troops burn a Seminole settlement in Florida in 1835 in this hand-colored lithograph published in 1837.*

OLA.

SOURCE EXPLORED

This lithograph of the Seminole chief Osceola was created by George Catlin in 1838. The previous year, Catlin had visited Osceola in prison, where he was being held for fighting U.S. troops. Osceola agreed to have his portrait painted. The following year, after the warrior died in captivity, Catlin made this lithograph based on his painting. It shows Osceola as a noble leader in his best clothes. Catlin spent a lot of time with Native Americans and was concerned that their cultures were being destroyed through expansion.

▲ Catlin visited Osceola in prison, but chose to portray him as a noble leader at the height of his powers.

On October 23, 1834, Chief Osceola addressed the Seminole people about why they had to resist U.S. demands:

❝ My brothers! The agent tells us we must go away from the lands which we live on, our homes, and the graves of our Fathers, and go over the big river among the bad Indians. When the agent tells me to go from my home, I hate him, because I love my home, and will not go from it. My Brothers! When the great spirit tells me to go with the white man, I go; when he tells me not to go. The white man says I shall go, and he will send people to make me go; but I have a rifle, and I have some powder and some lead. I say, we must not leave our homes and lands. If any of our people want to go west we won't let them. ❞

TRAIL OF TEARS

▲ George Catlin painted this image of Native Americans playing a ball game similar to lacrosse in Oklahoma, 1844.

In 1830, Congress passed the Indian Removal Act, requiring Native Americans to leave land east of the Mississippi River. Five years later, the U.S. Army began to force Native Americans on a journey of almost 1,000 miles (1,400 km) farther west. During the winter of 1838–39, more than 15,000 Native Americans from the southeastern states were taken to "Indian Territory" (present-day Oklahoma). With little food and no shelter on the way, as many as 4,000 people died. The Cherokee called the journey the "Trail of Tears."

George Catlin (1796–1872) kept a diary about his travels through the West and the time he spent painting Native Americans. He describes how Native Americans left their land when the white settlers arrived:

" I have seen [a Native American] set fire to his wigwam, and smooth over the grave of his fathers; I have seen him ('tis the only thing that will bring them) with tears of grief sliding over his cheeks, clap his hands in silence over his mouth, and take his last look over his fair hunting grounds, and turn his face in sadness to the setting sun—and I have seen as often, the approach of the bustling, busy, talking, whistling, hopping, elated and exulting white man, with the first dip of the plowshare, making sacrilegious trespass on the bones of the dead. "

◄ John Ross led political resistance against the removal of the Cherokee but was ultimately unsuccessful.

SOURCE EXPLORED

This print shows the Cherokee chief John Ross (Tsan-Usdi) in 1843. The document he holds is entitled "Protest and Memorial of the Cherokee Nation, Sept. 1836." This was Ross's request to the U.S. Congress that it should honor the treaties it had already made with his people.

THE TEXAS REVOLUTION

In 1835 American settlers in the Mexican state of Coahuila-Texas rebeled when the Mexican government abolished slavery. The rebellion led to the creation of the independent Republic of Texas. The Mexican general Santa Anna won a series of clashes against the Texians, as the people of Texas were known. However, the Mexicans were decisively defeated by General Sam Houston at the Battle of San Jacinto on April 21, 1836. Texas was no longer part of Mexico. In 1845, Texas joined the United States.

◄ *This image from 1912 shows a very idealized view of the last stand of the Texians at the Battle of the Alamo.*

SOURCE EXPLORED

This detail is part of an engraving made in 1836. It shows the Mexican general Santa Anna (right) surrendering to Sam Houston (left) after the Battle of Jacinto. Santa Anna denies having anything to do with the massacre at the Alamo. Houston replies, "Remember the Alamo!" and threatens to have him shot.

▶ *The cartoon was drawn in New York by Henry R. Robinson in 1836, soon after the Mexican surrender.*

Besieged inside the Alamo Mission in San Antonio with 189 volunteers by 2,000 Mexicans, William Barrett Travis wrote an appeal for help. The Texians all died in the Mexican assault on March 6, 1836:

“ I am besieged by a thousand or more of the Mexicans under Santa Anna—I have sustained a continual Bombardment & cannonade for twenty-four hours & have not lost a man. The enemy has demanded a surrender at discretion, otherwise, the garrison are to be put to the sword, if the fort is taken—I have answered the demand with a cannon shot, & our flag still waves proudly from the walls—I shall never surrender or retreat. Then, I call on you in the name of Liberty, of patriotism, & everything dear to the American character to come to our aid, with all dispatch... If this call is neglected, I am determined to sustain myself as long as possible & die like a soldier who never forgets what is due his own honor & that of his country—VICTORY OR DEATH. ”

MANIFEST DESTINY

In 1845, the *Magazine and Democratic Review* used the term "manifest destiny" to describe the belief that it was God's will that the United States should expand to the Pacific Ocean. The idea was not new. U.S. settlers had long believed they had a right to all of the continent. As slavery became more controversial in the East, many pro-slavery settlers used manifest destiny as a basis to argue for the creation of slave states in the West.

▼ *Emanuel Leutze painted* Westward the Course of Empire Takes Its Way *in 1861. It shows settlers heading into the bright, new world of the West.*

◀ John Gast's painting was typical of images that showed the "civilizing" influence of U.S. culture on the West.

SOURCE EXPLORED

American Progress was painted in 1872 by John Gast. It is an allegory showing America's modernization of the West. The angel is Columbia, who represents the United States. She holds a telegraph wire and a schoolbook, symbols of communication and education. The sky to the right is light; to the left it is dark, reflecting the unilluminated state of the West. Native Americans retreat before settlers whose methods of transportation reflects the history of settlement: walking, a covered wagon, a stagecoach, and a steam train.

AS THEY SAW IT

66 The far-reaching, the boundless future will be the era of American greatness. In its magnificent domain of space and time, the nation of many nations is destined to manifest to mankind the excellence of divine principles; to establish on earth the noblest temple ever dedicated to the worship of the Most High—the Sacred and the True. 99

–John L. O'Sullivan, who later created the phrase "manifest destiny," 1839.

WAGON TRAILS

▲ This hand-colored engraving was created in 1850. It shows settlers and a wagon train heading for California.

Pioneers headed west on foot, on horseback, by boat along rivers, or in wagons pulled by oxen or mules. From the 1840s, large numbers of pioneers formed convoys known as wagon trains to travel established trails to the West with a guide. A wagon train could travel 12 to 18 miles (20–30 km) a day. Most people walked alongside the wagons, which carried their possessions and the old or sick. The settlers also took herds of livestock with them.

◄ *This image reflects a romantic view of Native warriors as brave and defiant.*

SOURCE EXPLORED

This wood engraving was made in 1874. It shows the chief of a band of Native Americans forbidding a wagon train from crossing his territory. The chief's war spear is stuck into the ground. Perhaps it is a reminder that, if necessary, he will use force to stop the pioneers. In reality, Native Americans rarely attacked wagon trains, although they might form raiding parties to steal animals at night. This scene is therefore unlikely to have happened in real life. It probably says more about Americans' contemporary fascination with Native peoples.

AS THEY SAW IT

" A trip to Oregon with ox teams was, at that time, a new experiment, and was exceedingly severe upon the temper and endurance of people. It was one of the most conclusive tests of character, and the very best school in which to study human nature... People acted upon their genuine principles, and threw off all disguises. "

—Peter Hardemann Burnett, who moved to Oregon in 1843.

27

SETTLING THE WEST

The settlers who moved west needed places to live. In 1841, Congress passed the Log Cabin Bill. It allowed Americans living on the frontier to occupy land without purchasing it. They could build a cabin from logs or from turf, depending on the availability of trees. Congress wanted to encourage people to move west to ease pressure on the overcrowded East.

▼ This drawing from 1865 shows the famous one-room log cabin in Kentucky where President Abraham Lincoln was born in 1809.

SOURCE EXPLORED

This idealized view of a homestead in summer was created by the printmakers Currier and Ives in 1868. It was one of a set that showed the house in different seasons. It reflects the Homestead Act of 1863. The act allowed men and women over the age of twenty-one to claim 160 acres (65 ha) of land in the West in exchange for simply filling in a form and paying $10. This helped maintain the number of settlers heading west, but the process was already well underway. In the seventy years leading up to the act, around 700 million acres (283 million ha) of public land had already been purchased by private owners in the West, most since the Log Cabin Bill of 1841.

LAND RUNS

In the 1880s and 1890s, unoccupied land in what is now Oklahoma was opened to homesteaders. At a signal, huge numbers of settlers raced west in order to claim their own share of former Native American territory. These dashes to establish a claim to a plot were known as land runs or land rushes.

◄ The print shows a perfect scene in which animals are safely fenced in and a road keeps the settlers from feeling isolated.

THE MORMON EMIGRATION

The Mormons were a religious group whose beliefs, such as allowing a man to have more than one wife, made them unwelcome in the East where they were founded. In 1846, a group of Mormons headed west along the Oregon Trail to Iowa, and then south to Utah, where they founded Salt Lake City. From 1846 to 1869, more than 70,000 Mormon pioneers made the 1,300-mile (2,000-km) trek to their new home in Utah.

▼ This photograph from July 1847 shows an early Mormon wagon train about to enter the Salt Lake Valley.

◀ *This cartoon sets out both to mock the practice of polygamy and to suggest that Brigham Young is not a very good husband and father.*

SOURCE EXPLORED

This cartoon is entitled "The New Departure from Utah." It shows the Mormon leader, Brigham Young, fleeing from a mob of his wives and children. Americans were both horrified and fascinated by the Mormon practice of polygamy, when one husband has more than one wife. The cartoon reflects a long history of mockery of the Mormons. Ever since their founder, John Smith, claimed in 1830 that angels had given him two golden plates, the Mormons had been viewed suspiciously. The Mormons moved from New York to Ohio, Missouri, and finally Utah trying to find a remote place where they could practice their religious beliefs away from non-Mormons.

SALT LAKE CITY

When the Mormons arrived in Utah in 1847, it was still part of Mexico. Brigham Young said he recognized the Great Salt Lake Valley as the right place to settle because he had seen it in a dream. The Mormons began to build Salt Lake City, together with the Mormon Temple. They used extensive irrigation to make the arid valley suitable for farming.

THE GOLD RUSH, 1849

▲ This photograph was taken around 1849. It shows gold miners at their camp near El Dorado, California.

In January 1848 the discovery of gold near Sacramento, California, sparked a gold rush that spread across the country and around the world. California's population grew from 15,000 in 1848 to 100,000 in 1850 as more "forty-niners" arrived. In the event, few people made fortunes. More people made money from selling supplies to the miners than from finding gold. Most miners eventually ran out of money and found other jobs in California.

◀ The Way They Go to California *was published in New York in 1849. It reflects popular disbelief about the huge attraction of the gold fields in California.*

SOURCE EXPLORED

This cartoon from 1849 is entitled *The Way They Go to California*. It mocks the men rushing off to the gold fields. Men with picks and shovels are crowded on the dockside. Some dive into the water to try to get onboard a ship. Another miner parachutes from an airship, and a man also rides a rocketship.

Many prospectors soon lost their initial enthusiasm. Here John Eagle writes from California to his wife, Margaret, on June 13, 1852:

66 A person thinking of coming to California ought to consider whether he can stand to work all day, under a hot sun, up to the knees in water and mud, shovelling or pumping as the case may be; cook his breakfast, and be at work a little after sun rise; then cook his dinner at noon, and his supper at night, chop wood, bake bread, wash and mend clothes, &c.

If he is content to do all these things and run the risks of the journey, then he can come to California. If not, he is better at home. 99

THE OREGON TRAIL

There were two main routes to the West: the Santa Fe Trail led to California while the Oregon Trail led to the Northwest. The 2,200-mile (3,500-km) Oregon Trail started at the Missouri River and passed through present-day Kansas, Nebraska, Wyoming, and Idaho. Fur trappers and traders forged the trail between 1811 and 1840, and bridges and better quality roads gradually made the journey faster and safer.

▼ Daniel A. Jenks drew this picture of Cherokee Pass through the Rocky Mountains as he traveled the Oregon Trail in 1859.

Francis Parkman, a Harvard professor, wrote this account in 1846 of the trip he made along the Oregon Trail:

> "We were late in breaking up our camp... and scarcely had we ridden a mile when we saw, far in advance of us, drawn against the horizon, a line of objects stretching at regular intervals along the level edge of the prairie. An intervening swell soon hid them from sight, until, ascending it a quarter of an hour after, we saw close before us the emigrant caravan, with its heavy white wagons creeping on in their slow procession, and a large drove of cattle following behind. Half a dozen yellow-visaged Missourians, mounted on horseback, were cursing and shouting among them... As we approached, they greeted us with the polished salutation: 'How are ye, boys? Are ye for Oregon or California?'"

◀ Jenks drew a total of twenty-four scenes from the Oregon Trail. He sent them home to his sister, with a copy of his diary describing the journey.

SOURCE EXPLORED

This drawing was made by Daniel A. Jenks, who traveled with his family on the Oregon Trail in 1859. It shows two covered wagons being ferried on a raft across the North Platte River in central Wyoming. A camp has been set up on the far bank with three wagons and a tent, where a man with a long hook waits to help pull the raft close to the bank. Such river crossings were among the most dangerous parts of the journey west. If a raft overturned, families could lose all their possessions; they might even drown, as at the time few people knew how to swim.

THE COMING OF THE COWBOYS

At the end of the Civil War in 1865, Texas had around five million Longhorn cattle. Beef had become popular, and a new industry developed around the growing demand. Cowboys drove herds of cattle along one of four trails out of Texas to railheads in the north, from where the animals were transported to market. The job was hard and cowboys relaxed in rough frontier towns such as Abilene, Kansas.

▲ Cowboys of various ages sit on the ground near their chuck wagon during a mealtime on the open range.

◀ *Frederic E. Remington was the first artist to create small sculpted figures of Western characters. The form became so popular that similar figures are still widely produced today.*

COWBOY LIFE

Although Remington, Wister, and others created the myth of the heroic cowboy, in reality being a cowboy was one of the dirtiest, lowest-paid jobs of the time. Many cowboys were Mexicans; others were African Americans. They tended to be forgotten when cowboys became symbols of the values of "white" American life.

SOURCE EXPLORED

This sculpture is entitled *The Bronco Buster*. It was created in 1895 by the artist Frederic E. Remington. It shows a cowboy breaking in an untamed horse, which is rearing to try to unseat the rider. This was Remington's first sculpture, but he was already a leading painter of cowboy scenes. Remington and artists like him portrayed cowboys guiding their herds, fighting Native Americans, or exploring the wilderness. In 1893, Remington and his friend, the writer Owen Wister, collaborated on a book entitled *The Evolution of the Cowpuncher*. The book was the first portrayal of cowboys as American heroes, bravely facing hardship and discomfort. It gave rise to the whole myth of the Wild West that would be reflected in many more books and later in hundreds of Hollywood Westerns.

THE AGE OF THE RAILROADS

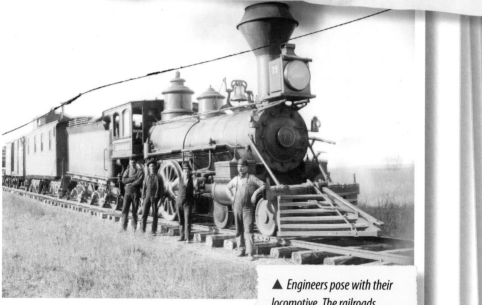

▲ Engineers pose with their locomotive. The railroads encouraged the creation of towns throughout the Midwest.

Soon after the invention of the steam locomotive in 1830, Americans planned a railroad across the continent. After a survey of possible routes in the West, the government gave away millions of acres of land to encourage companies to build the track. The first transcontinental railroad opened on May 10, 1869. It now took only eight days to travel from coast to coast, compared with six months by wagon.

◀ *This poster was created to advertise the services of the Rutland and Burlington Railroad in Canada in 1857.*

AS THEY SAW IT

❝ When they came to drive the last spike, Governor Stanford, president of the Central Pacific, took the sledge, and the first time he struck he missed the spike and hit the rail. What a howl went up! Irish, Chinese, Mexicans, and everybody yelled with delight. 'He missed it. Yee.' ❞

—Alexander Toponce, who witnessed the driving of the golden spike to complete the first transcontinental railroad in Utah in 1869.

SOURCE EXPLORED

This poster was issued in 1857 in Canada to encourage travelers to use the Rutland and Burlington Railroad. It promises a journey through beautiful scenery. In the eastern United States, railroads also competed for passengers. As the tracks headed west, they led to the creation of hundreds of new towns in the Midwest. The railroads also induced a boom in immigration. When westward migration slowed down in the late 19th century, however, so many railroads had been built that the falling demand meant many people who had invested in the railroads lost all their money.

LAST STAND AT LITTLE BIGHORN

By 1865, a few Native American tribes continued to resist forced removal to reservations. In 1876 the Civil War hero General George Armstrong Custer led the 7th Cavalry to force the Sioux and Cheyenne onto a reservation. On June 24, 2,000 Native warriors killed all 265 of Custer's men in the Battle of Little Bighorn. The battle was the last armed attempt to preserve the Native way of life.

▲ Charles M. Russell painted The Custer Fight in 1903. It shows Native American warriors charging the U.S. position.

SOURCE EXPLORED

This map of the battlefield accompanied a letter about the battle written by Robert Patterson Hughes to his wife on June 30, 1876. Hughes was an assistant to the expedition commander, Major General Alfred Terry. His letter suggests that Custer had acted foolishly by going into a fight against an unknown enemy. He had also disobeyed orders to wait for reinforcements. Despite this, Custer was still seen as a great hero, and his "Last Stand" became famous as an example of bravery and self-sacrifice.

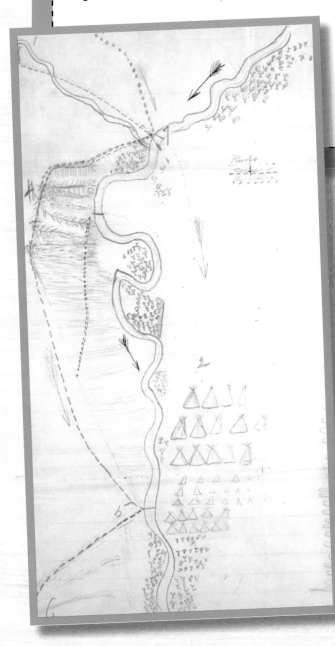

◀ *Hughes' map shows the Native American encampment, the Little Bighorn River, and the approach of the U.S. soldiers.*

DEATH OF A HERO

George Custer had become famous as a Union cavalry officer during the Civil War. His good looks, buckskin uniform, and long hair made him a dashing national hero. At Little Bighorn, however, he damaged his reputation by launching a poorly prepared attack on warriors led by the Lakota leader Crazy Horse. Custer's arrogance led his men to disaster.

A CHANGED AMERICA

▲ This view of New York Harbor from Castle Garden was created in 1887. It shows the new Statue of Liberty in the distance. It had been opened the previous year.

By 1850, the U.S. population had grown to 23 million. This number included Chinese immigrants in California, Mexican Americans in the Southwest, African Americans, including two million slaves, and Europeans. In 1850 alone, 300,000 immigrants arrived, mainly from Germany, Poland, and Ireland. Many headed west to claim their free land.

SOURCE EXPLORED

This illustration was drawn in 1866 and published in *Frank Leslie's Illustrated Newspaper*. It shows newly arrived immigrants at Castle Garden, New York City, which was the immigration center until the 1890s, when Ellis Island opened. At the top of the page, a ship arrives in the harbor. In the center, the immigrants are being registered. At the bottom of the page, they are leaving Castle Garden to begin their new lives. Passing through Castle Garden was not always straightforward, however. New arrivals were checked for diseases and examined about any political beliefs.

▲ The illustration shows immigrants being registered beneath signs in a range of European languages.

AS THEY SAW IT

❝ Farewell Castle Garden! I have met with nothing on the continent of Europe that can at all compare with the spectacle thou presenteth, and the benevolence and benefits that thou bestoweth: sacred asylum of the emigrant escaped from the dead ooze and dead lock of the Old World to the new life and progress, splendor and expansiveness of the New. ❞

—*The New York Times* article on Castle Garden, December 23, 1866

TIMELINE

1803	The United States buys 828,000 square miles (2,144,000 sq km) of territory from France in the Louisiana Purchase.
1804	Meriwether Lewis and William Clark set out to explore the North American continent; they reach the Pacific Ocean the following year.
1812	The United States declares war on Britain; the conflict ends with the British defeat at the Battle of New Orleans in 1815.
1819	Spain cedes Florida to the United States after U.S. troops have fought Native Americans in the First Seminole War.
1821	Mexico becomes independent of Spain; the following year Americans settle Mexican territory in Texas.
1829	The Baltimore and Ohio Railroad is the first major U.S. railroad.
1830	The Indian Removal Act allows Native Americans to be forced west to live on reservations.
1832	Some 14,000 Cherokee are forced west along the Trail of Tears.
1835	The Second Seminole War breaks out; it ends in 1842 with the removal of most Seminole from Florida. Florida is granted statehood in 1845.
1836	Texas wins its independence from Mexico, despite a defeat in the Battle of the Alamo. The first organized wagon train heads west along the Oregon Trail.
1841	The first wagon train arrives in California.
1845	John L. O'Sullivan first uses the phrase "manifest destiny."
1846	The U.S.–Mexican War breaks out; it ends in 1848 with U.S. victory. The United States annexes most of the Southwest. The United States agrees to set its boundary with Canada at the 49th Parallel west of the Great Lakes.
1847	The first Mormons arrive in the Salt Lake Valley, Utah.
1848	Gold is discovered in California, sparking a gold rush.
1853	Under the Gadsden Purchase, the United States buys the last pieces of territory in the Southwest.

1860	*Abraham Lincoln is elected president. Fearing that he will abolish slavery, South Carolina becomes the first state to secede, or leave, the Union.*
1861	*The Civil War breaks out between the Union and the Confederacy, which is formed by seceded states.*
1862	*The Homestead Act allows settlers to buy plots in the West very cheaply and easily.*
1865	*The Union defeats the Confederacy.*
1866	*The first cattle drive takes place when cowboys drive a herd of 260,000 cows to railheads in the North.*
1867	*The United States purchases Alaska from the Russians.*
1869	*The Union Pacific and the Central Pacific meet in Utah, completing the first transcontinental railroad.*
1874	*The invention of barbed wire allows ranchers to fence in large areas of the open range to keep livestock.*
1876	*At the Battle of the Little Bighorn in Montana, Lakota Sioux and Cheyenne warriors kill General George A. Custer and all his men.*
1877	*Crazy Horse, the victor in the Battle of the Little Bighorn, surrenders to the U.S. Army.*
1886	*The Statue of Liberty is opened in New York Harbor.*
1889	*White settlement is permitted in part of Oklahoma, which had previously been reserved for Native Americans. In the next decade, white Americans are allowed to move onto most designated Native American land.*
1890	*The U.S. Census Bureau declares that the Western Frontier has now been closed: the United States reaches across the whole continent.*

GLOSSARY

allegory A story or picture that can be interpreted to reveal a hidden meaning.

aquatint A colored print that resembles a watercolor painting.

cannonade A period of continuous artillery fire.

chuck wagon A wagon with cooking facilities used to feed cowboys on the open range.

engraving A picture made by drawing an image on a sheet of metal and using it to print on paper.

frontier The extreme western limit of settlement as the U.S. border stretched across the continent.

frontiersman A person who lives on the frontier, especially someone who is skilled in bushcraft and survival.

guerrilla Someone who fights using unconventional tactics, such as ambushes and raids.

homestead An area of land granted to settlers to build a house and outbuildings.

lithograph An image made by printing from a flat surface covered with ink.

manifest destiny A belief that the expansion of the United States throughout North America was both inevitable and justified.

navigable Describes a river or waterway that can easily be traveled by boat.

pioneer A person who is among the first to settle a new area.

plantation A large estate on which labor-intensive crops such as cotton, sugar, and tobacco were grown.

polygamy The practice of a man having more than one wife simultaneously.

range A large area of open land where livestock can graze.

removal The act of forcibly moving Native Americans from one region to another.

reservation An area of land put aside by the U.S. government for the use of Native American peoples.

sacrilegious Being offensive toward something that some consider sacred.

spike A thin, pointed piece of metal used to hold railroad tracks to ties.

Texian A citizen of the Republic of Texas.

FURTHER INFORMATION

Books

Collins, Terry. *Into the West: Causes and Effects of U.S. Westward Expansion.* Cause and Effect. North Mankat, MN: Fact Finders, 2013.

Crompton, Samuel Willard. *Lewis and Clark.* Great Explorers. New York, NY: Chelsea House Publishing, 2009.

Graham, Amy. *The Oregon Trail and the Daring Journey West by Wagon.* Wild History of the American West. Berkeley heights, NJ: Myreportlinks.com, 2006.

McNeese, Tim. *Early National America 1790–1850.* Discovering U.S. History. New York, NY: Chelsea House Publishing, 2010.

Morley, Jacqueline. *You Wouldn't Want to Be an American Pioneer! A Wilderness You'd Rather Not Tame.* New York, NY: Franklin Watts, 2012.

Wallenfeldt, Jeff. *From Democracy's Roots to a Country Divided: America from 1816 to 1850.* Documenting America: the Primary Source Documents of a Nation. New York, NY: Rosen Publishing Group, 2011.

Websites

www.nationalgeographic.com/ lewisandclark
National Geographic site about the Lewis and Clark journey, with an interactive log.

www. nps/gov/trte/index.htm
National Park Service guide to the Trail of Tears National Historic Trail.

www. america101.us/trail/ oregontrail.html
America 101 pages about the Oregon Trail, with maps, facts, and stories.

www.pbs.org/wgbh/amex/goldrush
PBS site to support the American Experience Gold Rush documentary.

Publisher's note to educators and parents: Our editors have carefully reviewed these websites to ensure that they are suitable for students. Many websites change frequently, however, and we cannot guarantee that a site's future contents will continue to meet our high standards of quality and educational value. Be advised that students should be closely supervised whenever they access the Internet.

INDEX